THE PLEASURES
OF LIFE AFTER 40

THE PLEASURES OF LIFE AFTER 40

by
Rex Curtis

drawings
by
James T. Pendergrast

BALLANTINE BOOKS • NEW YORK

Library of Congress Catalog Card Number: 85-91204

ISBN 0-345-32990-2

Manufactured in the United States of America

First Edition: April 1986

To Werner, without whom
this might have remained
another good idea.
     —R.C.

CONTENTS

At last—no more zits!

APPEARANCE/
CLOTHES

1—At last—no more zits!

2—Ironing one's hair is, largely, a thing of the
   past.

3—You've stopped waiting to become blond and
   gorgeous.

4—There just might be something to the Beauty
   Secrets of the Stars.

5—After all, what's another "character line"?

6—You can stop ripping out gray hairs, now that the darker ones are all gone.

7—The discovery of classic styles tempers your wardrobe somewhat.

8—What you once feared would be "permanent scars" have faded beyond recognition.

9—Shaving leaves less of a battlefield on your face.

10—Knowing there are certain things your hair just can't do avoids many haircut disasters.

11—Somehow the top hat and cane you bought in college seem less affected now.

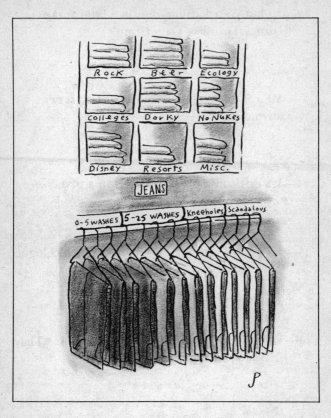

Your T-shirts don't require a filing system anymore.

12—At last your hairline dips in a little at the corners, just like Cary Grant.

13—Your T-shirts don't require a filing system anymore.

14—It's difficult not to look good in a tuxedo.

15—You know without a doubt how much cologne is *too* much.

16—You have a better idea of when the line "That … is *so you!*" is meant as a joke.

17—Growing a mustache is only a one-week project.

18—A small bustline has become more of an advantage, thanks to gravity.

You realize an occasional wardrobe crisis is no cause for alarm.

19—There is less of a tendency to attempt a complete tan in one day.

20—One feels more at home in cocktail lounge lighting.

21—Somehow one is less subject to censure for wearing really garish clothes (or even leisure suits).

22—The sales help at Bloomingdale's doesn't try to steer you toward a dress made entirely from one large industrial zipper.

23—You don't feel compelled to wear a new outfit immediately, particularly in a snowstorm.

24—You can resist buying a terrific secondhand sharkskin suit that is three sizes too large.

A truce is reached with the body.

25—You've given up *trying* to look older.

26—You don't bother trying to figure out why some people dress the way they do (for instance, a granny dress with hiking boots).

27—You have less disdain for *sensible shoes*.

28—You realize an occasional wardrobe crisis is no cause for alarm.

29—A truce is reached with the body.

30—It is no longer necessary to keep up with the world of Fashion.

31—If you didn't look great before, looking older is no worse.

DATING/
SEX/
RELATIONSHIPS

32—You notice that there's a difference between love being blind and love being deaf, dumb, and blind.

33—There is less guesswork in bed.

34—No one says, "I don't do that on the first date."

35—Romance is not expected to resemble "Love with the Proper Stranger."

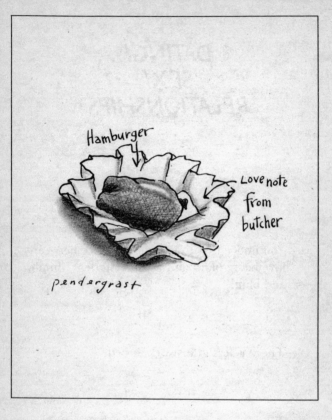

Hamburger

Love note from butcher

pendergrast

Romance is not expected to resemble "Love with the Proper Stranger."

36—The glamour of seeing a married man has worn thin.

37—There is less waking up Sunday mornings with an ink stamp on the back of one's hand.

38—It's probably safe to take the spare condom out of your wallet.

39—There is less waking up in a strange room with no memory of how one got there.

40—You can remember films seen at a drive-in theater.

41—One knows what to expect from blind dates.

42—You know several ways to handle the wrong person coming on to you.

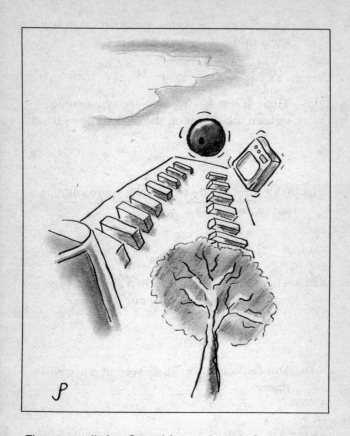

There is usually less flying debris at the end of a relationship.

43—"We must get together sometime" need not be taken at face value.

44—A shy teenage delivery boy may be grateful for lessons from an older woman.

45—Your friends who accuse you of robbing the cradle are more jealous than shocked.

46—It makes more sense to end a relationship *after* a birthday or Christmas.

47—There is usually less flying debris at the end of a relationship.

48—Pickup lines have become more polished.

49—Occasionally one forgets to use the pickup lines.

13

50—Whether you're desired for your looks or
your money becomes less of an issue.

51—You don't even try to remember phone
numbers that aren't written down.

52—The discovery that the Prince Charming you
met has capped teeth doesn't devastate you.

53—One has become more versed in subtle
distinctions, such as *shy* vs. *really not interested.*

54—It doesn't seem like forever when you wait
until Thursday to call someone you just met.

55—You can tell it would never work out with Mr.
X. at the laundromat, just by looking at his
sheets (cheap print).

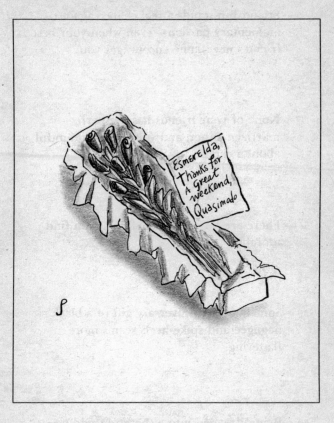

There are far more people that you find adorable.

56—Friendship stands a real chance against momentary passion—even when your best friend's new flame encourages you.

57—None of your friends has the perfect marriage either, and you're even doubtful about a certain royal couple.

58—There are far more people that you find adorable.

59—Somehow an anniversary gift of a black negligée and spike heels seems more flattering.

60—Being dragged into a shotgun wedding is unlikely.

61—You know that certain facts are best kept from a lover, like the details of bikini waxing.

You've learned that it's all right to be furious with someone you love.

62—New entries in one's address book first appear in pencil.

63—It takes much less time to go through the personals.

64—It's understood that _dynamic_ in a personal ad might really mean _pushy_.

65—The body is as fascinating as ever, even with slightly altered contours.

66—You don't have to worry about certain magazines being discovered in the underwear drawer.

67—You've learned that it's all right to be furious with someone you love.

68—The fear of public erections has passed.

69—There are a few things you could tell
  Cosmopolitan about how to handle men.

70—That someone is great in bed doesn't deter
  you from tossing them out, once you realize
  they're no good for you.

71—There's less of a mad scramble to arrange
  your face when you wake up next to
  someone.

72—More romantic opportunities appear in
  unexpected places (a pizzeria, a library, the
  same elevator at 8:55 each morning).

73—The idea of swimming into a riptide to get
  the attention of a lifeguard on whom one has
  a desperate crush is immediately dismissed.

74—You wouldn't dream of taking sides during a friend's marital dispute.

75—You can stand to be in the same room as the Other Woman.

76—Just as it wasn't true that all grownups were bigger and smarter, it's likewise not true that all twenty-year-olds are more desirable.

77—You don't bother to explain the bunny slippers to overnight guests.

78—It's occurred to you that total nudity may be less sexy than, say, a strategically arranged ostrich feather.

79—You realize you've never gone blind or gotten hairy palms, after all.

This time, romance is not wasted.

80—You don't have to fake a headache.

81—The temptation to call an old flame doesn't last too long.

82—Small talk is not necessarily without merit.

83—Heartburn is more frequent than heartache.

84—This time, romance is not wasted.

EXPERIENCE IS THE BEST TEACHER

85—Some things that were not funny then are *very* funny now.

86—There are several really dumb things that you've only done once.

87—Not every thought you have needs to be spoken.

88—You may not like what you're doing, but at least you know who you are.

You are not always taken in by the Dramas of Life.

89—You are not always taken in by the Dramas of Life.

90—One doesn't stop to answer rhetorical questions.

91—There is a greater willingness to compromise on nonessential details.

92—Time has taught that suspicion is sometimes wise.

93—A *pattern* begins to emerge in your dealings with supervisors at work, the police, your father, etc.

94—You know better than to tell your hairdresser *everything*.

95—It's understood that certain matters in life naturally fall into a Gray Area.

96—Fortunately, you recognize that the temptation to quit your job and become a Las Vegas showgirl has immediate obstacles in its path.

97—The idea of being a doomed poet and wearing all black seems slightly theatrical now.

98—One still has friends from the time of being a doomed poet and wearing all black.

99—You've learned that a good friend is not always someone you can live with—even for a week in a hotel room.

100—It takes much less time to identify flaky characters.

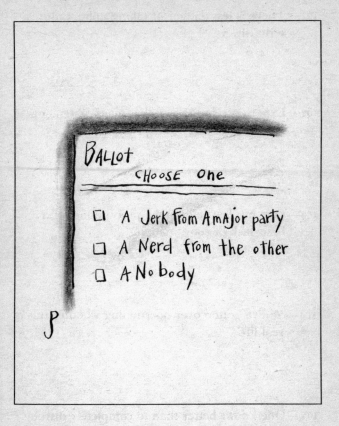

BALLOT

CHOOSE One

☐ A Jerk From A Major party
☐ A Nerd from the other
☐ A Nobody

There is less danger of taking politics too seriously.

101—There is less danger of taking politics too seriously.

102—Experience has shown that many statements are true in theory only.

103—One has learned to take precautions for a basic lack of coordination.

104—You've gotten over questioning whether this _is_ real life.

105—One knows better than to completely disrobe for a throat examination.

106—In the art of persuasion, you have an inkling of when to back off and stop talking.

107—You've learned that certain events can best be explained by a lapse into the Twilight Zone.

108—Some New Year's resolutions may survive the initial hangover.

109—You don't try to break more than one bad habit at a time.

110—The desire to be a cowboy has paled, now that you see some of the hidden drawbacks (eating canned beans).

111—Less time is spent arguing with someone who may not be right but is never wrong.

112—A wino collecting for Save the Children is unlikely to deceive you.

29

113—It takes less time to tell the difference between real information and a jive rap.

114—It's easier to distinguish between being in a rut and just temporary boredom.

115—Reflection on some of life's tragedies, like a backfired permanent, reminds one of what is Really Important.

116—You're more reluctant to fix what isn't broken.

117—In an idle moment you realize that schoolyard survival *did* help prepare you for Life.

118—There's a familiar point at which adding more spray starch will turn the shirts into stationery.

119—Some things are never forgotten, such as the exact shape of poison ivy leaves.

120—Even if you had been a baseball player, you'd probably be selling insurance or real estate now.

121—There tends to be less throwing out the baby with the dirty bath water.

122—Before you can set another arbitrary rule for yourself, an inner voice rebels with "Don't listen!"

123—Certain grudges that have been held for a long time begin to seem silly.

124—At some point it occurs to you that if Helen Keller could get through her life, then somehow you can get through yours.

125—One takes the time to find less drastic solutions to problems.

126—You're not so quick to give in to a professional martyr.

127—A momentary wish to be 25 or 30 is quickly cancelled when you realize what you would have to go through all over again.

128—You're old enough to appreciate some of life's ironies.

129—Cynicism is no longer a necessary part of your image.

130—Gradually one discovers there is a zen to many things, even folding the laundry.

Other people's motives become less opaque.

131—You realize the Peace Corps is best left as a daydream.

132—The mind seizes upon certain incidents (missing the boat, winning a jackpot) as statements of the Human Condition.

133—More often than not, you think before you speak.

134—Sometimes, you even consider whether the other person is actually listening.

135—One tends to linger less over misgivings from the distant past (such as never having been a cheerleader).

136—Other people's motives become less opaque.

137—You are more likely to recognize when it's time to give in and time to stick to your guns.

138—You know that some impulses are meant to remain just that—impulses.

139—It becomes easier to detect flattery.

140—You realize you would never have been happy as a ballerina, or an astronaut.

141—Self-pity has become boring.

142—You begin to suspect that maybe after all, happiness doesn't lie "over there."

143—Instead of feeling blue you call up a friend and dish.

144—When it feels as though your life is falling apart you know all you need is a really good facial or a massage.

FAMILY

145—The phrase "Because I said so" seems less unjust.

146—When your mother asks, "Aren't you going to Cousin Ida's wedding in Cincinnati?" you are able to say no with something approaching serenity rather than fear.

147—It occurs to you that, however bizarre, the things your parents did were somehow out of love.

The phrase "Because I said so" seems less unjust.

148—You know which Christmas gift will provide maximum annoyance to your in-laws.

149—You realize suddenly that you'll never really know why Uncle Waldo called you "Spot."

150—You can't remember the last time you tried to do your children's math homework.

151—There are certain topics you just don't discuss with your parents.

152—Having teenagers has made you bilingual.

153—The idea that in several ways your personality resembles that of one of your parents does not trigger an identity crisis.

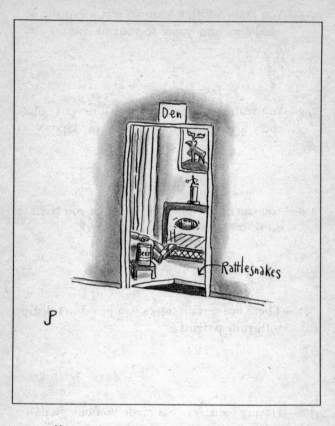

Your mother-in-law knows where not to tread.

154—It's just as well that children can never imagine their parents actually *doing* it.

155—If you haven't discussed the Facts of Life with your kids yet, it's probably unnecessary.

156—Your mother-in-law knows where not to tread.

157—Diapers are no longer a part of your reality.

158—Disposable diapers have recently become a part of your reality.

159—Raising someone's allowance pays for months (or at least weeks) of taking out the garbage.

160—It's still entertaining to push someone else's buttons.

161—You've acquired auxilliary tactics for winning an argument at home—like pointing out *who* selected the terrible motel on the last vacation.

162—It takes a really monumental temper tantrum to sway your better judgment.

163—During introductions, the host at a large family gathering doesn't feel compelled to mention the fact that you're "living in sin."

164—Competition with siblings has become boring.

165—The fear of having secretly been adopted has dissolved.

166—The plastic slipcovers at your parents' home can be removed, now that your children are nearly grown.

There is no one left who might say, "You look just like your Aunt/Uncle————"

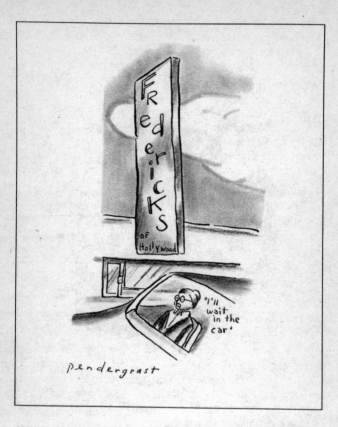

Your mother won't say a word now that you've decided to live your life as a blonde.

167—Children (one's own and others) provide a surprisingly cheap source of labor.

168—Your mother-in-law has learned that certain comments are not welcome.

169—There is no one left who might say, "You look just like your Aunt/Uncle———"

170—It becomes easier to view parenthood as an accomplishment.

171—You feel less ridiculous in a station wagon.

172—Your mother won't say a word now that you've decided to live your life as a blonde.

Threatening letters from creditors have to be more creative to intimidate you.

FINANCES/
POSSESSIONS

173—Certain items are no longer considered
 luxuries—champagne, for instance.

174—A silver candelabra has replaced the chianti
 bottles.

175—Threatening letters from creditors have to be
 more creative to intimidate you.

176—For someone who squeaked by in math,
 you've become a wiz at calculating tax
 deductions.

177—Participating in a month-long sleep experiment involving electric shock is no longer considered the solution to a cash-flow crisis. Neither is making a deposit at the sperm bank.

178—One is not too proud to hit upon a younger brother or sister for a loan.

179—The graduate school loans are paid in full.

180—When deciding to refurnish your home, thrift stores don't come into the picture.

181—You have a pretty good idea of what your limit should be at the roulette wheel.

182—The dangers of buying your way out of a depression have been amply demonstrated by experience.

183—Flashy sales are less successful at getting you to buy merchandise you don't want or need.

184—A close friend is not necessarily someone to whom you feel compelled to lend a large sum of money.

185—Your junk mail now includes unsolicited credit cards.

186—You have too many credit cards to be mistaken by the FBI as a dangerous radical.

187—It occurs to you that if your ship hasn't come in yet, it's time to get the tugboats.

188—There's still enough time to make an IRA worthwhile.

189—Odd hobbies (like collecting music memorabilia or refinishing furniture) have begun to bring in extra cash.

190—Artifacts saved from your childhood sell as valuable "antiques."

191—If you absolutely must, you can afford to fly to Vegas for the weekend.

192—By now, the orthodontist has been paid in full.

193—Raiding the closets provides enough merchandise for a profitable garage sale.

194—You don't think it's better to pay cash.

195—The verdict is in on whether candy bar theft would turn you into a hardened criminal.

196—The verdict is *not* in on exactly how you'll become rich and famous.

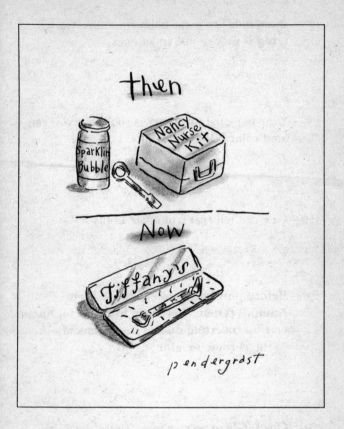

One tends to receive more useful birthday presents.

197—Diamonds are more likely on anniversaries (even if they're just small ones).

198—Your personal inventory is such that you can lend color TV's and cars.

199—One can tell real from *faux* Louis XV.

200—Before purchasing an expensive home Nautilus system, you begin to suspect it might end up collecting dust in the basement—next to the chrome weights.

201—One tends to receive more useful birthday presents.

202—A possible tax audit is of more immediate concern than feelings of alienation.

203—In comparing your accomplishments to those of, say, William Randolph Hearst, it occurs to you that he never had a budget for the dry cleaners.

204—You can cope with a gift that has a few strings attached.

205—You don't seriously argue with someone who offers to pick up the tab.

206—Not winning the Irish Sweepstakes is somehow less of a shock.

No one can stop you from having pizza for breakfast.

FOOD/
DRUGS/
BOOZE

207—No one can stop you from having pizza for breakfast.

208—It's possible to eat an entire plate of spaghetti without wearing the sauce.

209—You remember to turn off the spaghetti before it gets too relaxed.

210—Realizing you only live once, at times you throw caution to the winds and order an entrée like "Squid Supreme."

There is less genuine horror at discovering a hair in the soup du jour.

211—There is little guilt in not finishing an expensive meal that doesn't quite agree with you.

212—You can create several elaborate five-course dinners without using a cookbook.

213—It doesn't seem like such a great idea to add peanut butter to every recipe.

214—You're skeptical of diets promising twenty pounds a week in weight loss.

215—There is less genuine horror at discovering a hair in the soup du jour.

216—However, a hair plus something else is grounds for a lawsuit.

57

217—No amount of persuasion could induce you to enter a hot-dog–eating contest.

218—A three A.M. craving for vanilla ice cream and french fries makes you think twice.

219—When preparing a cheese sandwich, generally one remembers to remove the paper between the slices.

220—Peanut butter and marshmallow sandwiches are a thing of the past.

221—An unacceptable meal is sent back to the chef without guilt or fanfare.

222—The *positive* side of prune juice is discovered.

223—It's been a while since you went to The Four Seasons and drank from the finger bowl.

pendergrast

You can predict your body's reaction to a potent chili dog.

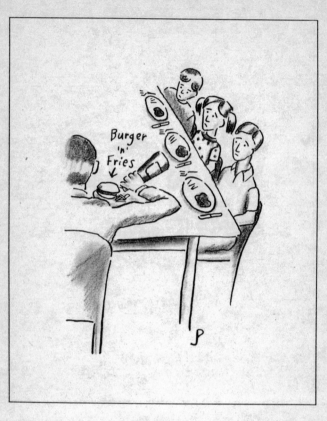

You don't have to eat liver.

224—You can predict your body's reaction to a potent chili dog.

225—You don't have to eat liver.

226—A friend's recipe for another hangover cure doesn't raise one's hopes too high.

227—One can refer to drugs by their actual names without sounding too square.

228—You can't remember the last time the doorbell rang and you flushed all your drugs down the toilet.

229—There is less ransacking of one's apartment after forgetting where the drugs are.

230—The Highway Patrol doesn't *automatically* assume the presence of drugs in your car.

231—There's an acquired skill at reading doctor's prescriptions, especially for Valium and Quaalude.

232—It occurs to you that no one has ever had a marijuana flashback.

LEISURE TIME

233—Halloween is still fun, if more elaborate.

234—You have several killer Scrabble words up your sleeve.

235—It's easier to trick oneself into not cheating at solitaire.

236—Becoming a Life Master at bridge is only a few trumps away.

Halloween is still fun, if more elaborate.

237—You can usually be a good sport despite losing Boardwalk and Park Place.

238—It is not true that a secret cult comes to brainwash you into Bingo Lust.

239—Needing less sleep means occasional party nights on, say, a Tuesday.

240—Cocktail party conversations tend to center more around *houses* and *cars* than *appearance* and *reality*.

241—On occasional weekends, the Movie of the Week is a perfectly acceptable substitute for dancing until two A.M.

242—You discover that you can still touch your toes.

243—That tennis is still preferable to shuffleboard leaves your self-image intact.

244—You can't be too out of shape to watch a football game.

245—You realize that in many ways bowling is the ideal sport.

246—The chair with the best view of the color TV is off limits to everyone but you-know-who.

247—A travel tour that includes a guide and planned activities doesn't compromise your sense of independence.

248—Round beds and mirrored ceilings do not exert undue influence in selecting motel accommodations.

249—One no longer apologizes for reading condensed books.

250—When you vacation in Europe you can leave the sleeping bags at home.

251—Your collection of hotel and airline silverware is virtually complete.

252—There's less peer pressure to go topless at Club Med.

253—You'd rather risk looking like a nerd under a beach umbrella than get a serious sunburn.

254—In times of boredom, you can always remember the summer you went skinny dipping with several girl counselors by convincing them you had "night blindness."

255—You get to pull apart the Sunday paper first.

256—Generally, one has already been exposed to
the hidden dangers of book and record clubs.

257—Sleeping late still has its rewards.

MODERN TIMES

258—The odds are against your being taken in by
a religious cult that insists on shaved heads.

259—Junk mail (or its absence) is taken less
personally.

260—Fortunately, foundation garments are not
nearly as cruel as during the Victorian era.

261—The ten breakdance lessons you got for your
birthday don't even rate a passing thought.

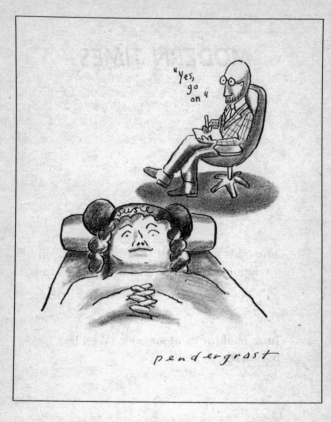

You tell the therapist you've grown up, and it's true.

262—It's hard to believe how much your house is worth on the current market.

263—Friends' divorces are less of a drain on one's checking account than their weddings were.

264—The calendar reminds you that you've already survived several Augusts without the therapist.

265—An inner voice guides you away from a new therapist whose theory is "Into each life a thirteen-alarm blaze must fall" (joking).

266—You tell the therapist you've grown up, and it's true.

267—Feminist issues aside, one doesn't mind being referred to as "one of the girls."

268—The friend who used to arrange Tupperware parties has turned to Marital Aid parties.

269—There's a greater tendency to feel that what people do in their own bedrooms doesn't really matter.

270—The willingness to question basic premises of one's life returns, like marching in the rat race.

271—The religious experience you've waited for comes—not at the chapel of Lourdes but at the Returns Desk at Saks.

272—Still rebellious, you'd rather be the Grandma in toreador pants than the one in the blue hair and a shawl.

273—Not that you're hoping for one, but you're _sure_ you could handle a stripping telegram with grace and dignity.

"NO PROBLEM"

274—The curse of the chain letter has never come to pass.

275—Having a "checkered past" is not necessarily a drawback.

276—It's easier to ignore what the neighbors think.

277—Sister Agnes might have been a little premature in her warnings about the path to Hell.

The curse of the chain letter has never come to pass.

278—No one will ever find out which altar boy put peanut butter on all the communion wafers.

279—When Sister Agnes's voice comments unfavorably on your leather wardrobe, you don't listen. Maybe.

280—It takes only thirty seconds to put in both contact lenses.

281—Meeting someone with the same dress at a cocktail party no longer requires a major scene.

282—A Saturday spent attacking the mildew is not viewed as a wasted afternoon.

283—You're no longer coy about letting people know exactly what you want for your birthday.

284—It doesn't matter who's watching as you fold your underwear in the laundromat, even the mail-order items.

285—The trauma of braces is but a dim memory.

286—A little eccentricity is considered part of the
territory.

287—Memorizing the Gettysburg Address is not so
difficult—now that you're on the coaching
end.

288—Certain episodes in your past have been
concealed by the passage of time.

289—A routine blood sample doesn't affect you
quite the way it once did.

290—It's been a while since the last time you had to
prove how cool you are.

291—The old recurring dream of finding yourself
back at school has lost its terror.

292—It's safe to assume that you won't go out and
spend your coin collection.

293—You don't have to worry anymore about what you'll be when you grow up.

294—Going to bed at ten P.M. doesn't make you feel as if you've given up adventure in life.

295—You can feel a killer headache coming on and know exactly how to nip it in the bud.

296—One is not tongue-tied when addressed by a plumber as "Babe."

297—Despite long tenure at P.S. 11, one is not a prime suspect in the Baby Ruth Extortion Ring.

298—When selecting a movie to see, whether or not you'll have to wait in line helps eliminate choices.

299—You've learned to cope with deadlines.

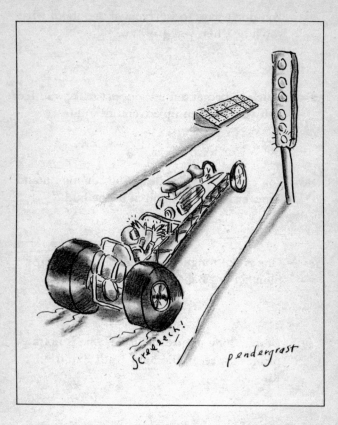

It's amazing what you can do without smudging wet nail polish.

300—Even in spike heels, you can run at a pretty good clip.

301—It's amazing what you can do without smudging wet nail polish.

302—You can tell white lies without missing a beat.

303—It's easier to control the urge to moon someone.

304—You're no longer troubled by superstition (knock wood).

305—In all likelihood you can install a dimmer switch by yourself.

306—Another funny car rattle does not cause a major upset.

307—One tends to be more philosophical about the misspelling of one's name.

79

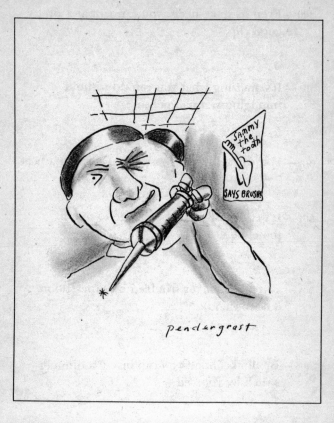

You'd rather ask for more Novocaine than be considered tough.

308—You'd rather ask for more Novocaine than be considered *tough*.

309—On reflection, only *parts* of your childhood were really terrible—like when the train set exploded.

310—It's been years since you passed all your exams, and no one has come yet to collect your firstborn.

311—Parallel parking is a veritable breeze.

312—An uncontrollable urge to try leopard print underwear is easily satisfied.

313—Less sleep is lost over what is, in fact, *normal*.

314—One can invent a logical explanation for almost anything.

315—It no longer matters that someone else can hear you in the bathroom.

316—It's possible to politely disagree, since deep down you know that you're right and they're wrong.

317—The mysterious red spots on your skin have come and gone before, so there's no cause for alarm.

318—A simple high-pitched scream has been found effective in alleviating stress.

319—It's surprising what friends will put up with.

320—You feel perfectly calm about disagreeing with a famous advice columnist.

321—Who's to say Mr. Bubble doesn't belong in a bachelor's apartment?

322—A wiseass doesn't usually get the better of you.

323—There is no hesitation in calling a spade a
      spade.

324—You have more patience when people explain
      in detail what you already know.

325—After putting your foot in your mouth, you
      know how to extract it graciously.

326—You're not too jaded to accept an insincere
      compliment.

327—The nude photo layout you once did is more
      cause for admiration than scandal.

328—You can say no without feeling the slightest
      bit guilty.

329—It doesn't take so long to think of comeback
      lines like "Selfish—moi?"

330—You have very little hesitation in playing a
      hunch.

There is more courage to live dangerously.

331—It's safe to assume that no one will ever discover who broke the gym window at North Larchmont Junior High.

332—The gypsy's prediction about murder and mayhem has never come to pass.

333—You've finally gotten over the time someone borrowed and lost your thesis notes on drug references in Disney movies.

334—No matter how long you stand on a street corner waiting for a friend, it's doubtful you'll be mistaken for a hooker.

335—It's easier to maintain one's poise, even under trying circumstances.

336—The past seems less terrible.

337—There is more courage to live dangerously.

ON THE JOB

338—It no longer takes a catapult to get you out of bed on Monday mornings.

339—A mere glance at the in-box lets you know exactly what kind of day it will be.

340—Unlike Jackie O., you don't do your own xeroxing at the office.

341—The word *pension* inspires joyous visions of a new lifestyle.

342—You probably *wouldn't* earn more waiting tables, even if you could negotiate the bunny ears and tail.

343—No one will know you went to see *Star Wars* instead of attending a business lunch.

344—You could give lessons in the art of covering your ass at work.

345—When it comes to typing tests, you're on the other side of the stopwatch now.

346—During an interview, one tends to think of better reasons for having left past jobs—such as *creative differences* or *a matter of honor*.

347—You can tell exactly when to tread lightly around your boss.

348—In the game of office politics you're already a senator.

349—Fewer lunch hours are spent devising original ways to spell your name or formulating your signature.

350—Among concerns at work, sexual harrassment takes a back seat to pension benefits.

351—Being called into the boss's office usually doesn't mean that termination is imminent.

352—One is more inclined to think twice before telling the boss what a jerk he is.

353—One might *be* the boss.

354—A quick tally of vacation, sick days, and holidays shows you only work ten-and-a-half months out of the year.

355—Expense accounts are a not inconsiderable source of income.

356—You know that getting plastered at the office Christmas party means you'll lose your chance to strike up a conversation with the new secretary.

357—On mornings when you literally fall out of bed, there's the thought that perhaps the office can get by without you for a day.

358—It occurs to you to see who else is in the office cafeteria *before* you speak.

359—The two-and-a-half weeks left before a vacation pass very quickly.

360—One is less apt to agree to deals that postpone an overdue salary increase.

361—Your approval is required on office memos, even for routine matters.

362—You've never regretted the decision to have a career.

363—It's never a problem to look busier at your desk than you really are.

364—You're not the first to be laid off during a slow period at work.

365—There is less embarrassment when discovered mumbling to oneself at work.

366—You know how to disappear briefly at the office after finishing a project at a quarter to five.

367—Between clawing one's way to the top and complete disinterest, the phrase "It's only a job" assumes more meaning.

368—You've gotten over the idea of "not going commercial."

369—New clients are not lost by your youthful appearance ("Can he really perform brain surgery?").

POP CULTURE

370—The "Important Art" you didn't understand is no longer discussed.

371—You notice that even Kim Novak no longer looks like Kim Novak.

372—Compared to James Dean or Mozart at your age, you're not doing so badly.

373—You haven't seen every movie nominated for an Oscar and it doesn't matter.

The "Important Art" you didn't understand is no longer discussed.

374—Like James Bond, you'll never say never again.

375—You don't think that life is more like a Bergman movie than a Fellini movie anymore.

376—Movie parents seem less pathetically misguided than before.

377—There isn't the least embarrassment in crying at the movies, unless you're watching *The Poseidon Adventure*.

378—It's possible to view stag films without lust and appreciate their unintended humor.

379—You've become indifferent to the love life ups and downs of even a favorite rock star or movie personality.

Before accompanying a friend to a gruesome horror movie, a voice asks, Do I really want to see this?

380—Instead of inventing an elaborate excuse when asked to attend a twelve-hour experimental Swedish film, you just say, "I don't think so."

381—Like Scarlett O'Hara, you know there are certain things not worth thinking about until tomorrow.

382—One is more resolute about walking out on a bad movie—even one on the VCR.

383—A life of crime has lost its glamour, especially if you've seen enough women's prison movies.

384—Before accompanying a friend to a gruesome horror movie, a voice asks, *Do I really want to see this?*

385—You don't ask yourself Serious Questions about your own marriage when watching "Divorce Court."

386—Joan Collins wasn't an overnight success, either.

387—You notice that even though Captain Kirk lost some hair and physique, somehow *he* went on living.

388—You don't ponder song lyrics for the Meaning of Life.

389—You don't have to go into suspended animation when *that song* comes on the radio.

390—The fear that Rolling Stones records would turn into Perry Como records overnight was unfounded.

391—The breakup of the Beatles has become less traumatic.

392—Among your friends there are fewer heavy-metal fanatics.

393—It is possible to appreciate both Jane Austen *and* Jackie Collins, though differently.

394—An earnest book on tips for teens provides hours of amusement.

395—Astrology doesn't inspire you to rash decisions.

396—You can guess which friends wouldn't laugh at Ethiopian or dead-baby jokes.

397—The allure of having designer initials everywhere has faded.

398—You're not really expected to learn slam-dancing.

399—You feel comfortable using several foreign phrases, such as: *cabernet sauvignon, ersatz, sushi, puta, database, et cetera*.

400—You still like Van Gogh, but Hockney or Rauschenberg is more your style for a role model.

401—The idea of youth-obsessed culture provides grist for a lively conversation.

402—You finally understand existentialism (though you still can't explain it to someone else).

403—It doesn't bother you that the same figurine you call an objet d'art is considered by someone else to be a chatchke.

404—If "ring around the collar" were *really* a threat to your marriage, it would've ended long ago.

405—The Barbie Doll you could never part with has become a collector's item, especially the Hawaiian Vacation Wardrobe.

406—Even Gidget is over forty.

407—You've been around long enough to tell Alfie
what it's all about.

If you were so inclined, there are probably several people you could blackmail.

REVENGE OF TIME

408—At least one teen idol you hated has fallen on hard times.

409—An old college roommate who always made you feel inferior turns up at a career-burnout seminar that you're leading.

410—If you were so inclined, there are probably several people you could blackmail.

411—You learn that the swim team captain has lost his hair and physique.

You learn that the swim team captain has lost his hair and physique.

412—Belated confessions about the past clear up
some events that were always puzzling.

413—Your children are old enough to recognize
that you were right about a few things after
all.

There is no such thing as a term paper.

THINGS YOU NO LONGER HAVE TO PUT UP WITH

414—There is no such thing as a term paper.

415—There isn't a single item in your wardrobe that you're expected to grow into.

416—Others have given up trying to change you.

417—The decade of *living up to your potential* has passed.

418—Having a bad cold does not include Vicks Vap-O-Rub on your chest or rectal thermometers.

No one expects you to shovel the snow.

419—You no longer pretend to like certain things.

420—No one expects you to shovel the snow.

421—Phone calls from friends feeling desperate at three A.M. become less frequent.

422—Nicknames coined by classmates (like "Shorty" or "Piano Legs") have been forgotten.

423—Hazings are definitely a part of the past.

424—You no longer have to pretend that high school was the best time of your life.

425—Now that you've forgotten the last of your high school French, you can stop telling yourself that you *really* should reread Proust.

426—There is less peer pressure to be cool.

427—No one presumes to question what you wear.

pendergrast

Some of the instruments of past humiliation have been vanquished.

428—Being drafted is out of the question.

429—Some of the instruments of past humiliation
have been vanquished.

430—No one suggests that you need a haircut.

431—When was the last time someone asked if
your were reading *Being and Nothingness?*

432—PMS will soon be a welcome deletion from
your life.

433—You don't have to deal with anyone snapping
a towel at your ass in the locker room.

434—You will never again have to walk door to
door selling Girl Scout cookies.

MISCELLANEOUS

435—*Jr.* has been replaced by a *II* at the end of
one's name.

436—Birthday cakes require just one symbolic
candle.

437—Children are sinfully easy to impress.

438—You discover you can still play the clarinet
(even though your last lesson was thirty years
ago and it was never your idea in the first
place).

439—Many statements can be made by simply raising an eyebrow.

440—Mrs. Stern, who gave you an *F* in behavior in second grade, meets an untimely end.

441—Sometimes you don't bother to be "nice."

442—Due to a certain authority in your voice, your view is taken seriously on subjects you know nothing about.

443—There are more of those moments when you don't argue with *the way it is.*

444—Others have also considered how sorry everyone will be when they die, too.

445—It appears to the casual observer that you know exactly what you're doing.

446—Judging simply from the times you've said, "May lightning strike me if..." there must be a guardian angel keeping tabs.

Mrs. Stern, who gave you an F in behavior in second grade, meets an untimely end.

447—There is no mystery about *who* and *whom*.

448—A few snappy lines, like "*Quel* bum-*mer!*" have mercifully bitten the dust.

449—*Gray* has largely been replaced in your vocabulary by *salt and pepper*.

450—Sometimes after cheering up a friend, it occurs to you that you *do* matter, Dr. Carl Sagan notwithstanding.

451—The suffering of the rich and famous, as reported in supermarket tabloids, reminds one that the grass is not always greener.

452—Deep down, there is still a part of you that wants to be perfect.

453—Friends have already let you know whether or not it's a good idea for you to sing outside of the shower.

454—Living arrangements that include a roommate are probably by choice.

455—It takes little effort to convince people that you've got it all together.

456—By now enough quotes come to mind to impress someone in conversation:
—*Yeats*: "Your important arguments are with yourself."
—*La Rochefoucauld*: "We can tolerate those who are boring, but not those whom we bore."
—*Wicked Witch of the West*: "I'll get you, my pretty, and your little dog too!"

457—You're more adept at reading people's faces, especially the killer smile.

458—It doesn't matter that you never learned how library books are catalogued.

459—Double entendres do not fall on a deaf ear.

460—There is more than a passing interest in pursuing certain abandoned goals.

461—Hearing about acts of heroism can still be inspiring.

462—You can distinguish between someone who doesn't appreciate something and someone who puts down *everything*.

463—You don't bother to "straighten up" before the cleaning person arrives.

464—It's still amusing to study someone who doesn't suspect they're being observed.

465—It's not always necessary to be in the fast lane.

466—By now, even the least mechanically inclined can have an intelligent conversation about car repairs.

467—There probably are still some surprises ahead, and becoming president of the PTA had better be one of them.

468—It's never too late to take the veil.

469—Many incidents can be excused by Mid-Life Crisis.

470—Others begin responding to the threat of being forgotten in your will.

471—By now you can bullshit your way out of almost anything; the more serious, the better.

472—"Life is short" justifies several projects, such as getting a tattoo.

473—All of a sudden you realize you can't think of one person under forty who won the Nobel Prize.

474—Tolstoy never even *started* until long after age forty.

475—Instead of demonstrating for a cause you mail a check.

476—There are cities like Miami Beach to make you feel underage.

477—Fifty doesn't seem especially old anymore.

478—You know that a foreign film that confuses you probably confused the screenwriter as well.

479—It's been pointed out that romantic fantasies about one's doctor are commonplace.

480—You've become adept at overhearing certain conversations.

481—Reincarnation seems more and more plausible.

482—The fundamental things still apply.

483—Arm wrestling can still settle disputes in your favor.

ABOUT THE AUTHORS

REX CURTIS attended Hunter College. As well as being an artist, he has published short fiction and poetry in small magazines and has worked for several years in the publishing business. He is an avid skateboarder and lives in L.A. Contrary to his better judgment he is at work on a novel.

JAMES T. PENDERGRAST was born of poor but noble stock in Douglas, Arizona, a small town near the Mexican border, on "the night the Douglas Drugstore burned down," December 15, 1944. When little James was eight years old, his family moved to Fullerton, California, where he was forced to endure schooling and puberty, often at the same time. After receiving his B.A. in Art and working a year toward an M.A. at CSU Fullerton, he left school to make his way in the world.

Since 1977 he has been plying his artistic talents in New York City, an activity which has led him recently to claim the Universe as his art piece, saying he "found" it while riding on a bus in downtown Manhattan.

On the
Lighter
Side...